M000107606

Copyright © 2018 by Rainbow Hospice and Palliative Care
Second edition 2018

All rights reserved. This publication may not be reproduced, reprinted, copied
or otherwise transferred digitally or mechanically in any way without the
express authorization of Rainbow Hospice and Palliative Care.

Design: HDG Design Group, INC.

For information please contact:
Rainbow Hospice and Palliative Care
1550 Bishop Court
Mount Prospect, IL 60056

www.RainbowHospice.org

TABLE OF CONTENTS

PREFACE

The television personality Fred Rogers once said, "Love isn't a state of perfect caring. It's an active noun—like 'struggle.'"

The same can be said, I think, of grief. The death of a loved one is a life-changing event for all of us, but is especially fraught for a child, innocent of the random misfortunes of life, and not yet mature enough to comprehend the depth and complexity of permanent loss.

In *The Road to Good Mourning*, Rainbow Hospice's Vicki Scalzitti offers an invaluable resource for parents and guardians faced with the overwhelming task of guiding their children through the process of loss and healing. Vicki, an accredited crisis and trauma specialist, has counseled thousands of grieving families over the past thirty years. Since 2005 she has also managed Rainbow's Good Mourning program for bereaved children, teens, and families.

I read *The Road* in a single sitting, captivated. Every chapter, every page of the book resonated with me. I lost my father as a boy, at a time—the mid 1960s—when there were no grief counselors, no support groups, and no trove of self-help books to navigate the surviving spouse through the long, rocky shoals of parenting a bereaved child. Everyone assumed our father's death was just one of life's tragic events, and that we would deal with our loss as best we could and move on. And so we did.

But in fact I never confronted my grief at all. I simply nudged it into some dark corner of my mind, where it festered silently, only to strike back in the most insidious ways and at the most unexpected times. My attention span shortened, my grades suffered, and in my teens I became uncharacteristically belligerent, fighting at the slightest provocation.

Reading this book, I saw myself in chapter after chapter—or to be more precise, I saw the absence of myself: If only my mother had known about this approach...if only she had explained things that way. Perhaps then I could have more easily made my way through the confusing swirl of emotions—shock, sadness, anger, fear—that engulfed me after the tragedy.

One bright summer day a man I didn't know appeared at our door and informed us that our father had died. He had suffered a massive heart attack and was gone before the ambulance arrived. He was 42 years old. I was ten. It was the first and only time I saw my mom cry. My three sisters and I circled around her, and we embraced and wept as a family, less one.

Some survivors compare the death of a loved one to a wound that never heals. Some compare it to a scar. Others describe it as a hole—a hole in the heart, in the soul, in their life. I prefer C.S. Lewis's metaphor: "The death of a beloved," he wrote, "is an amputation." My father was a hero to me. I looked at him in awe. He could ride a horse, he could play the piano by ear, he could juggle four oranges at once, he could even fold a sheet of paper into the shape of a bird whose wings would flap when you tugged on its tail. He taught me how to pitch a baseball and how to catch a football. Most of all, he was a loving husband and a caring dad.

It wasn't until two decades after my father's death that I began to comprehend the value of good mourning. At the age of thirty-one, upon the birth of my son, I had an epiphany of sorts: it dawned on me that I had spent my entire adolescence blaming my father for leaving us, for hurting my mother, and for tearing apart our happy family life. It was an irrational thought, untrue and unfair, but it was, perhaps, a typical reaction of a ten-year-old kid traumatized by the sudden loss of a beloved parent—the anguish of an amputation. Without even realizing it, I had nursed this anger like a low-grade fever, for years. In *The Road* we learn that one of the toxic byproducts of childhood loss is anger. And resentment. And acting out. I was batting an imperfect three-for-three.

The Road is replete with astute yet practical advice any parent can follow. It offers, among many other things, a step-by-step approach to sharing the difficult news with the child; a list of the ways grief can affect a child's physical health; and a concise summary of how best to communicate—and therefore commune—with our kids throughout the journey toward recovery.

Vicki's guidance is neither glib nor pain-free. Sometimes it is counter-intuitive. We should, she enjoins us, use direct language when talking about the deceased. Don't say daddy is sleeping now, or that he is no longer in this world. Tell them he died. We should also share with them the story of their loved one's death. Children are naturally curious to know what happened, and such knowledge is a meaningful part of the healing progression.

Memories are important, too, but not just the good ones; relating bad or hurtful memories is a key step in the easing of emotional distress.

The Road to Good Mourning is based on modern research in childhood bereavement. It is steeped in compassion and understanding, and is expressed through the sage lens of one who, herself, has suffered profound personal loss. If the road to good mourning begins with love, perhaps it ends with forgiveness. To reach that endpoint, there is much you can do. Start by reading this amazing book.

Clayton Bond
Volunteer, Patient Care and Comfort Care
Board Chair
Rainbow Hospice and Palliative Care

INTRODUCTION

For over 35 years, the Rainbow Hospice and Palliative Care mission statement – "Empowering our community to live with hope and resilience throughout the journey with illness and loss" – has been our absolute and steadfast commitment to our patients, their families, and all those who love and care for them.

To serve patients and families dealing with terminal illness, we have offered continuing support through Grief & Loss Services. We've developed many ways to assist people on their journey through life-changing loss – regular memorial services, support groups, workshops, counseling, and support from volunteers who have experienced loss themselves.

In 1995, Rainbow Hospice and Palliative Care made a special commitment to grieving children by providing a home and staff for the *Good Mourning Program for Children, Teens, and their Families*. Good Mourning offers comprehensive services – through support groups, family camps, special events, and school partnerships – to Rainbow Hospice patients' families and to the community at large. Good Mourning, founded in 1988, was the first program of its kind in the Chicagoland area and has served more than 3,000 children and their families in its over thirty-year history.

If someone you love is now seriously ill, your concerns are focused on your loved one and how you will all get from where you are today to the end of the journey, how you'll take care of him or her and how you'll navigate the next few hours, days, weeks, or months. For many families receiving sad and life-changing news about a loved one, the question, "Now what do we tell the children?" follows closely – adding another layer of concern and burden.

We offer this collection of articles to those caring for children as they come to terms, perhaps for the very first time, with the tremendously big and universal issues of life – and death. The chapters come from educational pieces that were written for parents and guardians of the grieving children who attend the Rainbow Hospice and Palliative Care **Good Mourning Program**. Families have told us that this information helped them care for their children through a difficult experience:

- How to help children find their voices

- Explaining the effective and clear ways to talk with them about an illness and death

- Finding meaningful ways to include children in the family experience

- Understanding better how children respond to stress and how to respond to them

- Discovering together that even a big experience can be broken down into manageable pieces

- How to provide security and supportive structure in children's everyday lives.

We hope that this book will help you as well.

Over the years, countless grieving children have shown us that grief does not have to stop anyone from becoming exactly who he or she is meant to be. Out of a grief journey, children and families can grow into greater resilience, confidence, and compassion, taking the gift of their loved one's life into a bright future.

That is our hope for you.

Vicki Scalzitti
Manager, Family and Community Education
Rainbow Hospice and Palliative Care

CHAPTER 1

TALKING WITH KIDS:
THE CHEAT SHEET

Talking with children about life and death doesn't come naturally to most of us... Sharing difficult news with them can seem daunting.

Kids are supposed to be exempt from these difficult realities, aren't they? But when someone we – and our kids – love is seriously ill, suddenly illness, life, death, and why bad things happen to good people are exactly the topics for a much-needed conversation. As parents, we feel like there is so much riding on our "getting it right" for our children.

"Getting it right" isn't as hard as it sounds. There's a sensible, step-by- step process for talking with our kids. The first task is focusing on what kind of information our kids need and giving them the information in a way that is appropriate for their level of understanding.

The second task is maintaining realistic expectations for ourselves and for them. We can't stop our children from being sad about what is looming ahead for the person they love and for themselves, because that is not a realistic goal. If we believe it's our responsibility to find the "magic words" that will help our children understand what is happening and also keep them from experiencing sadness about it, we'll never get to the conversation.

Even when the news about a loved one is dire, most children are better off when they understand what's happening and what to expect. Kids often don't ask the questions they have unless we give them a specific opportunity, inviting them to talk with us by initiating the conversation. Children feel concerned when someone they love is becoming sicker and changing right before their eyes. If we're not talking with them about what they're seeing, they may come to believe that talking is "off limits" and carry their anxiety around silently, as an increasingly heavy burden.

Some families believe that keeping children away from the patient/loved one is best, that the kids "shouldn't see him like this." Most children know that something is wrong if they're kept away from someone they love and who loves them. They can wind up feeling worried, isolated, and excluded.

If they're too young to wonder about why they're not seeing someone who has been an important part of their lives (or if they didn't see the person regularly enough to experience the separation as unusual or different) the death, when it happens, can seem very shocking and mysterious. Many children say that seeing their important person when he/she was very ill was a good thing – they understood better that it was the right time for the person to die because they could see that he/she was too sick to stay.

Finally, children, just like adults, need their opportunity to say "I'm sorry" or "I love you" or "Goodbye." Without it, they can feel left out or cheated, emotionally at "loose ends."

Besides being better for our children, talking with them about a loved one's illness and prognosis can prove to be better for the whole family. We don't have to be as concerned with someone "letting something slip out" or having the kids overhear a conversation not intended for them, which is never the best way for a child to get information. Worrying that a child may hear something he/she is not supposed to hear is stressful for everyone involved.

When kids are feeling anxious and left out, their coping strategy may be (intentionally or unintentionally) to get attention by being whiny, oppositional, or regressive – speaking "baby-ishly," having pottying accidents, or relentlessly clinging to a parent. These behaviors cause escalating stress for everyone, especially difficult if the parent(s) is also the patient/loved one's primary caregiver.

The "Cheat Sheet" on the following pages is a how-to for sharing difficult news. You will do what you feel is right for you and your children and that is as it should be. Each of us will find our own way to talk with our kids, depending on their ages and our own personal way of communicating with and responding to them.

We hope that you'll consider including them in the experience of saying goodbye to someone they've loved, because it can be an important emotional passage in their lives. Although it may seem daunting, this is a precious opportunity: to teach our children; to let them know we are always solidly "in their corner;" to make ourselves available to them at a difficult time; to relieve their fears and anxieties; to share our beliefs; and to explore together one of the great and profound mysteries of the human experience.

The Cheat Sheet

Begin by finding out from the child what he has observed, been told, or figured out.

- This invites the child into the conversation, gives her "ownership" of the conversation, and allows the child to demonstrate what she already understands (or believes) about what is happening.

Find out what the child knows about illness and death.

- Has she experienced a death before?
- Has he seen something on TV or read about death?
- Keep in mind the prevalence of death as a topic in children's movies and literature. (E.g., Disney movies are full of references to death – *Snow White, The Lion King, Bambi, Coco, Finding Nemo,* etc.)

Share with the child "what can happen if" by asking her about different scenarios and outcomes.

- What can happen when people get very sick or have_____?
- Do you know what happens if a person can't get better?

Actively help the child to develop and ask questions.

- Ask him about changes in the patient's appearance or the way the patient acts.
- Ask her about medical equipment, medication, and procedures.
- Be prepared to answer/address the child's questions and concerns.

Don't focus all your attention on whether or not the child "gets it."

- Understanding is a process, something that people grow into over time.
- Having the story about what has happened or will happen is empowering, even if not fully understood.

Normalize hard feelings – being afraid, sad, guilty, worried.

- Name your own difficult feelings and tell what makes you feel the way you do.
- Ask the child what hard feeling(s) he might be having.

Affirm for the child how her own heart, spirit, and talent will help get her through difficult times.

- An artist can communicate how he thinks and feels through his drawings. Making music on the piano is a good way to show how you feel.
- A reader can get books about people being sick (or having died) and then share with other people what she has learned.

Identify the go-to person/people for the child.

- This may be someone other than parents, especially if parents are stressed or overwhelmed.
- Ask the child if there is someone he would feel comfortable talking to.
- Make sure that the person chosen is willing to answer questions and provide support.

If you would like more information or some assistance, please call:

The Good Mourning Program for Children, Teens, and Families at Rainbow Hospice and Palliative Care **847-653-3140** or contact us through our website, **www.RainbowHospice.org/Grief-Loss/Support-for-children-and-families/Good-Mourning**

CHAPTER 2

A CHILD'S GOODBYE
CHILDREN AND FAREWELL RITUALS

Working in hospice, we often talk with children who are anticipating or grieving the death of grandparents, and increasingly, great-grandparents.

They share stories about the importance of these enriching relationships. Children appreciate the warmth, patience, and unhurried attention that older relatives so lovingly provide. Older people take time for children - a great gift in today's hurry-up society.

In addition to the grandparents who have the luxury of spending special time with their grandkids, many grandparents today are co-parenting their grandchildren or providing for their day-to-day care while parents work. Children respond to the depth and wisdom that folks one generation (or more) removed from them bring to their lives.

Today, many more children than we might expect experience the death of a parent. Social Security statistics indicate that by age eighteen, almost one in twenty children has lost a parent. Conservatively, that translates to one child in every classroom. Children lose siblings as well, and although the percentage whose brother or sister dies is relatively low, sibling loss is a life-changing passage for the children who experience it.

Increasingly, children may also be impacted by the loss of expected siblings – baby brothers and sisters who die before or at birth. Many years ago, pregnancy was barely mentioned to children (until the change in Mommy became glaringly obvious) and going to the hospital and coming home with a new baby was very mysterious. Now prospective big brothers and sisters listen to the baby's heartbeat, attend "Big Brother, Big Sister" classes, and visit the birthing center, all in preparation for welcoming the new little one.

When something goes wrong with a pregnancy or at the time of birth, siblings may feel frightened, confused, and disappointed. If there will be a funeral or memorial service for the baby, there may be questions about brothers and sisters attending.

It may seem easier to leave children out of farewell rituals. Wakes and funerals are long and tiring. For adults in mourning, having to make all the arrangements, greet all the visitors, and find the time to say their own goodbye can be stressful.

- Realistically, should they also be expected to take care of the children – especially little ones?

- Do children belong at wakes, funerals, memorial services?

- Do they understand?

- Could they be traumatized by such a close encounter with the physical reality of death?

It is almost always true that when a person who is significant in the life of a child dies, a child needs to say goodbye. It's the first significant step in a healthy and manageable grief experience. The benefits of saying goodbye and being included in the farewell ritual are great and far outweigh our concerns.

The following suggestions may be of help as you plan to include your children in this very important family event.

- If at all possible, let children see the person who has died. This can happen at home (if the person died there), at the hospital, at the funeral home (a private viewing by special arrangements with the funeral director), or at the wake/funeral.

  ▸ Explain to children where they will see the person and how the person is different, e.g., he isn't breathing anymore, he can't hear you or talk to you anymore, she can't move now, etc.

  ▸ While we often agonize over whether or not the person looks like him/herself, most children tell us the person looked fine or okay.

  ▸ If children have questions about changes in the person's appearance, answer them with enough information to be accurate. Too much information is not helpful.

- Use the correct language - "Grandpa has died" or "Grandma is dead." Avoid using euphemisms such as "has gone to sleep" or "We lost Nana."

- Let children view the person from the distance that is comfortable to them. Allow children to touch or talk to the person who has died, but do not prompt them or insist that they do.

- Children who are old enough may be included in funeral arrangements.
  - Even very young children can choose the kind of flowers they would like to give and may bring the flowers with them.
  - Older children can do readings or assist with music selections.
  - Many children write a letter, draw a picture, or choose a keepsake to put into the casket.
- Prepare children for what they will encounter at each step of the farewell ritual.
  - Explain what the funeral home, church, and/or cemetery look like.
  - Explain and name significant elements such as casket, hearse, or grave.
  - Include an explanation of how people may behave and help children to understand that the tears of the adults around them are okay and nothing to be afraid of.

When they're well-prepared and know what to expect, children will not be overwhelmed. Many kids are positive about the wakes and funerals of the people they love, enjoying the chance to talk and hear stories about their loved one, visiting with and receiving support from friends and family, and feeling glad to be included in such an important event.

It can be helpful to designate a close friend, family member, or babysitter to accompany the children throughout the wake and funeral, a person who can see to it that children are fed, supervised, and attended to. He or she can make sure that children, particularly younger ones, get necessary breaks – going to a park, a restaurant, or home. Sometimes children must leave a wake early in order to get a good night's sleep or simply because the day becomes too long for them.

The person acting as the child's advocate can answer his/her questions and be aware of the child's emotional state when parents are busy with the demands of the day. While interaction between parents and their children is an important part of the wake and funeral, the attention to the children that the advocate can provide assures parents that their children are not "lost," physically or emotionally.

After all the careful explanations, arrangements, and planning, a child may decide herself not to attend a wake or funeral. In this case, the best way to proceed is to ask if there is something particular that is frightening or worrisome. If there is, try to allay the child's fears and concerns. Next, make sure the child understands that this is the last opportunity to see the person who died and to be together with others in the family as they say goodbye.

Offer alternatives – attending only part of the events, having a limited time during which the child will attend the wake or funeral, viewing the person's body or not, etc.

Don't argue or insist that the child attend or express disappointment if she decides not to participate. Ask if there is anything she would like to do: sending a note or drawing a picture that a family member will put into the casket, choosing flowers for the person, lighting a candle at home, visiting the cemetery at a later date, taking a plant to church or planting one in the yard in memory of their important person.

Grief often looks very different in children than it does in adults. While some children may be tearful and sad, many more tend to play and socialize their way through the farewell ritual. Many children have called the wake, "That big party we had for Grandpa."

Children really connect with the gathering aspect of these events and they lead the way when it comes to celebrating a life. They often recount the wonderful things said about the person who died and talk about all the people who came to the funeral. Children will remember having been part of the important goodbye and are affirmed by participating.

With thoughtful preparation, we can safely and meaningfully include children in our farewell rituals – a precious opportunity we have to share with them what it means to be family.

CHAPTER 3

THE MOST IMPORTANT STORY EVER TOLD

For almost every griever, sharing the story of what happened to the loved one is the very beginning of a long and complicated healing process.

This is different than memory sharing or talking about the important person's life: it is the story of his or her death. For children, understanding the cause, circumstances, and events that make up the story of the death of their important person is the foundation of their grief experience. Re-visiting what happened as time goes on and as she grows and changes is also critically important for a child living with life-changing loss.

- Having a story that he understands and can share with others is the first step in the child's grief process. Children who do not understand, at an age-appropriate level, the circumstances surrounding the death seem unable to move into further processing and resolving other aspects of their grief.

- By listening to how fully or accurately a child chooses to share the story, we may find out how comfortable (or not) she is — whether a difficult or complicated story is making the child feel vulnerable or worried about acceptance and the reactions of others.

- Telling the story provides the opportunity for the child and parent(s) to re-examine the events and discover when new information is needed — when the child's developmental changes have prepared him to receive different or more detailed information about the death. Since the story must be age-appropriate, it will change over time to reflect a child's growth and understanding.

The events around the death of their important person can feel very confusing, disconnected, and disordered for some children, especially if the death was sudden or complicated (a homicide, suicide, accident, or substance abuse-related loss). Often, there was not adequate (or any) opportunity for them to "get their arms around" what was happening because everything seemed very chaotic. Some kids were too young to make sense of what was occurring or to form memories of the events.

Even if a child understands everything she needs to understand about the death when she is three, that doesn't mean that the same story will make adequate sense when the child is seven or twelve or seventeen. The "right" story for a growing child is not a destination: it's a moving target that changes as he grows, requiring more detailed information, re-working, and re-grieving. To accomplish this, our children will revisit the story and need us to support them and answer their questions as they discover what else they need to know.

Although it is generally true that a child who can tell the story is empowered by doing so, it's also true that some children are less forthcoming. Just like adults, some kids are more private than others. Keep in mind that every death is expressed in many stories: there is the story that belongs to a parent, a spouse, or a sibling and each child has his or her own.

For every death, there is also the "public" story and the "private" one – the things that happened that are part of everybody's reality and the things that happened to each of us on the "inside." No matter how much a child chooses to share (or not to share), it's important that his need to know and understand is met with truthful, age-appropriate information when he needs it. A child should have confidence that questions are accepted and will be dealt with honestly and without a lot of drama, that she has open and generous permission to ask the questions she needs to ask — today and tomorrow.

It's important to listen carefully and respectfully to stories children share. Sometimes there are incongruities in a kid's story, something that isn't true or may be confused. It's best not to challenge or correct a child or attempt to "straighten him out." If your child seems honestly confused, it may take some time for him to understand more clearly what happened to the person who died.

You can help this along by asking gentle questions and sharing your recollections of what happened. If a child is reluctant to share or continues to change details of the story because she clearly chooses to do so, we have to respect that choice. Everybody has a right to her own story — and to decide when, where, and with whom she will share it.

It can help children to think about their story in parts – the scariest part, the saddest part, the part that helped the most, etc. It can also be helpful to share the story in sequential pieces: first, tell about what was happening before the person died; next, let's tell how we each found out the person died, etc.

By telling the story in "parts" or "pieces," children come to understand the complexity of the experience and realize how many different feelings they have about it. Telling the story, one element or event at a time, helps a child identify where he may be missing vital information, where she may have been confused, where he may be forgetting things about the events. "Bite-sized pieces" can also make the story feel less overwhelming and more manageable.

Another way to make the story more manageable is by introducing "something else to do" while telling the story. "Busy hands" help some children to feel more in charge of their emotions and reactions as they talk about a very difficult time. Drawing is a good tool. Modeling clay is another: kneading it, shaping it, punching it, and warming it are all tactile outlets for the strong physical images and feelings that children can experience while they re-visit and share the events surrounding their important person's death.

For many children, drawing, writing, singing, or some other form of expression may be the best way to tell the story. As human artistic expression has demonstrated for tens of thousands of years, not every important story is shared in words.

While we may want to shelter our children from some of the harsher realities in the stories of how our loved ones died, it's better to protect our children **with** the truth than trying to protect them **from** the truth. Secrets are a hazard to everyone.

Please don't let your children find out something significant about their important person's life or death from a cousin, a neighbor, or an over-heard phone conversation. No one will work as hard as you will to make sure your children get sensitive and important information in a way that is safe and supportive.

It can be hard to know how much to tell and when. Perhaps the best way is to listen to your children's stories and offer to answer any questions they might have — in an age-appropriate way. Their questions indicate how much detailed information they are ready for at the time.

Try to stay on the side of truth. You can always provide more information as they grow, but it's very difficult to take back an untruth — and it can damage your children's trust in you.

Keep in mind that littler guys may be telling about what they heard happened or what they imagine happened. It's good to have an accurate story, but

some story is much better than no story at all! There is always time to get things straightened out as they grow and learn and change.

If you have a little one or if your child was pre-memory (under 4—5 years of age) when his or her important person died, part of your very important job is to keep telling the story!

We hope that your kids will choose to share their story with you (but we strongly **discourage** demanding that they do or acting disappointed if they don't). Although a lot of healing can take place within a family as these important stories are shared, it's best to let your kids be in charge of what, where, and when they choose to share. It's important to provide the opportunity for them to talk about the death of their important person — and to offer it again and again — but it's also important to respect that sometimes their answer is "no" or "not right now."

The Story begins when a child finds out that something has gone terribly wrong and ends a few days after the rite of farewell. This is the story that profoundly changes a child's life and we are privileged to bear witness to it. The challenge for grown-ups who love and care for a grieving child is to open our ears, our minds, and our hearts to him — to listen, reflect, accept, and affirm her as she grows to understand.

CHAPTER 4

GRIEF IS A PAIN

Grief is a normal life experience, although a difficult and painful one.

Grievers, big and little, can wind up with a lot of issues and concerns about their bodies and their physical health. For your children, the loss they're experiencing may be their very first encounter with serious illness and death.

Many kids do not have access to medical professionals to answer their questions at the time of their loved one's death. Even for kids who have all their questions addressed at the time, grieving and growing means there may be new questions as they reach each new developmental stage.

As they grow, children are ready for more details. They know more and have heard more about illness, accidents, and death, so they relate some of that information to their own experience, trying to sort out what applies to their important person.

You and your kids may have questions about yourselves or others in your family. Kids often have questions about other peoples' stories that they've heard. Some have questions about the things that are all over TV news — medical breakthroughs, new diseases, or celebrity deaths.

The Internet, used judiciously, is a great source of information (and some significant misinformation) for many of us. In addition, your own physician or pediatrician may be willing to take some extra time to talk with your children, especially if you have it scheduled into your appointment (or schedule your appointment at a time of day when your physician is more available to take some time).

Parents may feel challenged by their children's sudden desire to know more or to question what they were told about their important person's death. If you find yourself confronted by questions about what you told them (or didn't tell them), the best answer is a simple one — "When you were younger I told you what I believed you could understand at the time. I answered the questions you asked me. Now you're more grown up and I'll tell you more because you can understand more, and I'll answer the questions you're asking now."

While most of us will think about the physical body in regards to the people we've loved and lost to death, we often neglect thinking about our own physical well-being. If someone we love was very ill, and particularly if we were caring for him/her, we may have become too caught up in what was happening physically to our loved one to pay attention to ourselves. Maybe it was just too time-consuming to take notice.

When our very important person was ill, and since he or she died, our kids are also going through a lot and might be feeling whiny, tired, low-energy, and "sniffly" all the time — or may be having tummy troubles that come and go at an alarming pace. These are called vague physical complaints and bereaved children experience them regularly. The complaint or hard-to-pin-down symptom is often a child's way of expressing some kind of pain, usually emotional. It's a way of letting us know that something is just not right, and certainly, it isn't.

It's important to understand that although we recognize that grief is an emotional experience, grief actually happens on a lot of levels: it has emotional, psychological, and spiritual dimensions. Grief happens in our bodies too, often in ways that we miss because we didn't expect that "feeling grief" actually means something physical.

Upon hearing the news that something or someone significant is lost to us, we may have a visceral reaction. The word "visceral" refers to "viscera" – meaning related to our organs. That's pretty physical. When people receive difficult or traumatic news, they can experience pounding in the ears, that sinking feeling in the gut, or heart palpitations. All of those are due to the triggering of the human "fight or flight" response that happens when we feel threatened.

How grief affects us physically, in the long run, is hard to quantify and report statistically. With humans, it's very difficult to get a control group – a group of people exactly like the grievers we want to study, but who aren't grieving. People have an incalculable number of variables. When we grieve, we bring everything we are along with us, so it's almost impossible to compare a group of grievers to non-grievers and assess what exactly is physically different about grievers.

Some studies and anecdotal reporting suggest that general health plays a part in responding to grief, as does lifestyle. Diet and exercise still count in the mix. So does how we handle our relationships and emotions: isolated people are more at risk for physical complications when they grieve and so are the "strong, silent" types. We know that there are physical changes associated with grief. The information that comes from general surveys might not withstand scientific scrutiny, but it does raise some interesting issues about grief and our physical health.

First, grief can be dehydrating. While tears represent very little actual fluid, the production of tears takes much more fluid than the amount of tears we shed. So if we're tearing up regularly many times a day, we can get dehydrated. In addition, grievers may forget about (or just not pay attention to) drinking or eating. Dehydration is bad for the brain and can cause (or worsen) feelings of sadness, exhaustion, confusion, and helplessness. Grievers need WATER, WATER, WATER and less caffeine, bubbly, sugar-filled, or alcoholic beverages.

Second, grief is exhausting. Grief is very wearing and can cause sleep disturbances, messed up REM and sleep cycles, restlessness and "night moving." People who have been widowed may sometimes experience "empty bed syndrome," trouble falling or staying asleep alone. A grieving child often wants to sleep with a parent, a sibling, or just not alone in his/ her own room. Some kind of shared sleeping arrangements occur in over 70% of families with children who have experienced significant loss.

Third, grief causes changes in nutrition, generally not positive changes. Managing food can be a source of stress. There are issues surrounding the time and effort involved in shopping, cooking, and cleaning up – especially for those who are stressed single parents. Depressive over-eating, desire for mood alterers like caffeine, sugar, and (more dangerously) alcohol can become issues for many of us.

Fourth, grievers, little and big, seem to have suppressed immune systems and get sick more often, not unlike when we experience any other significant stressors.

Fifth, many grievers will be more accident-prone, perhaps from sleep problems, inattention, or trouble focusing.

Sixth, many grievers wind up over-medicated, getting the wrong meds, and taking them for too long. While it may be appropriate for a primary physician to prescribe a short course of antidepressants or medications for anxiety or sleep problems, use of these medications for more than six months should be monitored by a psychiatrist. They specialize in making sure a person gets the best drug and right dose for the symptoms they're experiencing. Careful monitoring assures safety and getting the best results.

It's important to note that grief in children can manifest in many ways that look like depression, ADD, ADHD, or anxiety. *Before children are diagnosed and/ or medicated, it's important to get a thorough evaluation by a professional who is fully aware and informed about the child's loss experience.*

Seventh, many grievers will not get adequate medical care and monitoring of their health. Some people feel they don't have the time to get to a doctor or have nobody to make them go! Sometimes the loss (of a spouse, a job, or income) triggers a change or loss in medical benefits for a whole family.

The physical effects of grief eventually subside and most adults experience improvement, usually beginning at 6 – 9 months after the loss. At eighteen months after the death, most people are approximately as physically healthy as they were before the loss.

After a loss, children usually rebound faster physically than grown-ups do. If after four to six weeks your child is not eating well, not sleeping normally (most nights), is still having (new or different) pottying regression or accidents, complains of tummy or headaches or **seems genuinely uncomfortable at any point,** it's time to seek assistance, starting with the primary care physician.

Some of this may sound familiar to you. We hope this is useful information and that it can be of help to you, your children, or someone you care about. While we often think about getting over grief or getting out of it, grieving is an important process in the experience of human life. Grief contains the seeds of its own healing, and, like other kinds of healing, it happens at its own pace and in its own time.

CHAPTER 5

LIFE AND DEATH...
AND DRAGONFLIES!

We all know the butterfly's story of generation and transformation, the whole "egg — larvae — chrysalis — beautiful" thing.

Probably fewer of us routinely think of the dragonfly's journey as a metaphor for change and metamorphosis. The dragonfly's life cycle, however, is equally useful as a symbol and metaphor for ours!

Changing, transforming and "becoming" are pretty abstract concepts for children to grasp. Ironically, kids may find it hard to see change because they are always in the change process themselves. It's all they know, yet we see it so clearly in their lives with each passing day.

They're becoming taller, faster, stronger, more verbal (or less, if it's a teen age boy we're talking about). They grow intellectually and emotionally. Even their experience with life-changing loss is growing and changing with them. They are bringing it along with them, understanding it differently, wanting to understand it more, anticipating all the ways it makes their lives different from other kids' lives. They begin to consider the real "Mysteries of the Universe" as well — where is my important person who died, what might he be like now, what does she have to do with my life today?

While we often think of insect lives as relatively fleeting, the dragonfly in its "nymph" stage actually lives under water for 3 to 4 years. Eventually, the nymph leaves the water and crawls out onto some plant where it sheds its body and discovers a whole different body that has been developing inside. That body is nothing like the one before, and this one can fly! The metaphor resonates with most of us, particularly as we think of the people we have loved and lost, wondering if they have come into being in another way and another place, entirely different than they had been.

Perhaps the reason that most of us can wonder and imagine about transition after life is because we're already used to thinking about, observing, and experiencing change and transition as part of life. It happens to our kids daily, it happens (perhaps more subtly) to us, it happens to our parents and other older folks in our lives, and we end this life experience with the most dramatic and heart-rending transition of all.

Little guys need to learn the facts of life. For preschoolers through 8 — 9 year-olds, the topics are pretty basic — how lives begin and change and end. Bigger kids (pre-adolescents from 10 through even young adults in their early twenties) are taking a more universal and expansive view. Why is there life and death? How is my life like others and how is it different? What happens to people when they die? What will I be like when I'm grown? If my important person who died was here now, what would he or she tell me about my life or their own? Kids are looking at life — both the small, personal picture and the huge, ongoing, universal picture as well.

Some important facts and facets of "life cycles" that are important for children to understand are:

- What happened to the important person in our life who died is not what happens most of the time (when the death is that of a young parent or sibling).
- While each individual life has a beginning and an ending, life itself continues.
- The people we've loved continue on in us – influencing our physical selves, who we are, what we think, what we do.
- Life re-creates itself as we live out experiences that are like those that were also part of the life of the very important person who died.
- Loss, change, healing and regeneration are part of life.

The story of the dragonfly — its beginning as an egg, its water-bound nymph stage, and its soaring, shimmering dragonfly existence — is wondrous and miraculous. And so is every individual life and life itself.

The book *Lifetimes*, by Mellonie and Ingpen, opens with this simple and profound statement,

"THERE IS A BEGINNING AND AN ENDING FOR EVERYTHING THAT IS ALIVE. IN BETWEEN IS LIVING."

That about sums it up!

CHAPTER 6

SUNNY, WITH A CHANCE OF STORMS

Feelings — a mystery, a force, a quagmire, ephemeral, powerful, the place we may lose ourselves, and the way we can find ourselves again!

While "how we feel, what we feel, how something makes us feel" is often a focus of grief work, it takes more than saying what you feel to cope with what you feel. Expressing feelings is a crucial step, but only the first step.

For the youngest grievers, the primary task is identifying and naming feelings. They need a working vocabulary for feelings that may seem to be bigger than they are. With little ones (three through kindergarten/1st grade), it is best to keep it simple:

- Ask them to identify feeling faces and make feeling faces — Can you show me your sad face? How does this face [and then you, the grown-up, make a face] look like I'm feeling?

- Read stories about feelings, listen to poems, and sing songs about feelings.

- Talk about the feelings they like and the ones they don't like as much — use the words "good feelings" and "hard feelings" (not **bad** feelings, since we don't want kids to think some feelings aren't acceptable).

- Ask, "What makes you feel...?" — to help young children identify feelings as a response to what happens in their lives (i.e., little children do not always understand that they may still be sad about something long after it happened).

As kids grow, feelings can become pretty complicated stuff. As you may have experienced by now, some kids don't want to talk about their feelings ever. Others avoid talking at times — usually when they're acting as though they really need to talk about their feelings and simply refuse.

A certain number of kids like to talk all the time, sharing their feelings and memories easily and often. For many children, a big stumbling block to talking is emotional vocabulary: it's hard to talk about feelings that don't have a familiar word association to you. Talking about "sad," "mad," or "glad" may be easy, but "frustrated," "anxious," "relieved," or "guilty" is not so simple.

When we talk about feelings with our kids, we help them to develop their emotional vocabulary, to attach words to feelings. Feelings that are layered and complex can be difficult to name. How can we be glad that someone has died because everything was so hard and sad when he/she was sick and still be worried about what will happen to us? That's not an unusual conglomeration of feelings for a grieving child, however for the child it can be new and confusing.

Listening and responding, asking gentle questions and repeating back what you hear your child say are effective ways to talk about feelings. Suggesting that, "There are words for when we feel like that" – and sharing them – helps a child feel understood, smarter, and better equipped to explore the "fuzzy" emotional world.

A younger child may be concerned about having been angry or impatient with the important person who died, wondering whether her own "bad" thoughts caused the person harm. Assure her that our thoughts don't hurt people and that everybody gets angry (or impatient or frustrated) sometimes.

Older children and teens often feel guilty about the very ordinary adolescent conflicts they got into with their important person who died. All kids, little and big, can be very relieved when we let them know that, throughout our lives, being angry with someone doesn't mean that we don't love him/her.

Children sometimes "act out." If your child appears to be over-reacting, you might try to look at his behavior through the "grief lens." Grief is not one feeling. It's a process of experiencing many different feelings: sadness, yearning, anxiety, worry, anger, disappointment, frustration, guilt, relief, and hopefulness.

Sometimes these big feelings spill over for children, coloring their reactions and responses to other, seemingly unrelated, situations. A young child whose Grandpa died suddenly may be much more afraid of the dark or of Mommy leaving the house to go shopping than he was before, leading to crying, howling or "tantrum-ish" behaviors.

Teens seem to be naturally frustrated a lot of the time, and a grieving teen can become even more so – yelling about how "nothing is fair" or "nothing ever goes right." When your child seems exceptionally sensitive, vulnerable, or angry, it may be his grief rearing its head. Responding as calmly as we can is most helpful: "I know you're angry right now, but you seem angrier than I'd expect you to be about your team losing the ballgame. You're usually a very good sport. Is something else bothering you right now?" or "I was thinking how much your Dad would have liked to see you play and it made me feel sad and mad that he couldn't be here. How about you?"

Sometimes the story about what's so hard about being a grieving kid will come spilling out. Other times we get shut down entirely. In either case, it's worth remembering that our kids are grieving and that grief is not always neatly contained or clearly expressed.

While children need to have their emotional reactions understood and accepted — to be told that it's okay to cry, to be afraid, to worry, or to be angry — sometimes it can seem that they're "playing the grief card." Occasionally kids, big and little, use "being sad" or "missing him" as an excuse for less-than-desirable behavior. If that seems to be the case, it's an opportunity to re-frame the situation for your child and set reasonable expectations for her behavior.

- I understand that you're sad because _____ died, but right now I think you're unhappy and angry about not having a friend over because I'm too busy.

- It's okay to feel angry and let me know that you do, but not okay to hit or call names.

- It's okay to feel disappointed and to tell me that you are, but right now "no" means "no" until another time. Whining and yelling until you get your way is not going to work, and I don't appreciate how you're acting right now.

- Always end by saying, "If you do want to talk about missing _____, I have time for that — and I'll always make time for you when you need to talk."

Sharing examples from your own experience (or modeling) builds trust and makes it possible for your child to see feelings and emotions as acceptable and manageable. Modeling grief is a process of picking and choosing what we share with our children, being honest about our sadness or frustration, and accepting our own feelings. When we do this, we normalize our own grief and theirs as well.

Grieving children often experience increased anxiety and concern. They worry about us and, especially in the case of parental loss, can feel frightened that they may not be taken care of if something happens to their surviving parent. Kids need to be assured that we will get better — that we won't always be this sad and that we can still take care of them.

Some expressions of adult grief are too powerful for our children to witness, so we need support from other grown-up family and friends as we vent those feelings. When deep grief takes over and we grown-ups hit a low (or loud) point, it's better for everybody if we hang on until our kids are taken care of and out of the immediate vicinity. It can be too frightening for our children to be exposed to every facet of our powerful adult grief.

One of the mystifying things about a child's emotional state is how quickly it seems to come and go. A child can be sobbing and crying for the person he lost and then asking for a fruit roll-up moments later. Even big kids are quick-change artists when it comes to feelings: they're sad, frustrated, or hopeless one moment and texting (LOL) with friends the next.

The Dougy Center in Portland, Oregon (the very first program for grieving children in the United States) characterizes children's emotional responses to loss as coming in "grief bursts" – relatively short periods of time, usually just minutes, when a child feels her grief intensely. A very short time later, everything is back to "business as usual." This is how children normally experience significant grief, not an indication that they don't actually grieve or don't grieve deeply.

Finally, children are more emotionally open at certain times during their day. Bedtime, when they're tired, is a prime time for a grief burst, convenient or not. Transition times also seem to trigger grief for many children, resulting in crying or angry outbursts as they're getting ready for (or being dropped off at) school, when they have commitments or appointments, when it's time to finish dinner and move on to homework, etc.

Dealing with a grief burst requires patience and tolerance. It's much easier to respond to our child at times like this than it is to try and push him through it. The good news is that, with a little compassionate attention from us, the storm usually passes pretty quickly.

Speaking of storms, sometimes "playing" our way into talking about feelings is inviting to kids, and weather is a great metaphor for talking about grief. Like the weather, our grief comes and goes and changes constantly. We can't control it, and we have to adjust and prepare ourselves to deal with its requirements. All of us can identify our "sunny" moments, our "cloudy" thinking, our "lightning" temper, or "rainy" moods. But, just as certain weather doesn't provoke the same response in all of us, the same is true with our kids.

While foggy days make some of us feel uncertain and vulnerable, others revel in the blurry quiet. Sunny days are cheerful for most of us but can feel scorching and glaring to some. Lightning is scary to a lot of people but exciting for those who enjoy all the noise and fireworks.

When you invite your kids to share their "weather" feelings with you, don't assume that what their "inside weather" means to them matches your ideas exactly – or even closely. Finding out what makes your child feel "rainy," "sunny," or "stormy" and sharing what makes you feel "breezy" can be a lot of fun for both of you and can give you important insights into how your child is viewing, expressing, and coping with his/her emotions.

There are other ways to talk about feelings that are fun for kids. Colors make a great metaphor and feelings associated with color run throughout our language: "tickled pink," "green with envy," sad and "blue" are just some examples. Just as the weather metaphors are personal and individual, every kid will have her own answer for the question, "What makes you feel orange?" – but each answer is interesting and an invitation to talk more about "the color you feel."

Children who find it difficult to talk about how they're feeling can do other things to express and manage their emotional state. Clay is a great medium for pounding, molding, and squeezing – a good physical outlet for sadness, frustration, and anxiety. Shooting hoops and other physical play can help children discharge the energy associated with strong feelings. Some kids like to draw the things they are having trouble putting into words and some find it helpful to make or listen to music. Dealing with the many feelings that accompany the experience of life-changing loss doesn't always require talking. Playing with a child as she works her way through the experience can be very affirming and reassuring.

At times, grief seems to "hibernate" in children, going underground and seeming irrelevant to their lives. After a long period of relatively normal functioning, a child may suddenly start talking again about their important person who died, asking questions about what happened, telling stories about the person or asking us to tell them stories, crying or moping or complaining that what happened was not fair.

Just like grief bursts, this is part of the normal grief process for children. It occurs as a child grows and develops – as he sees the loss through more mature eyes. A child at three may understand what happened in her life in a way that is complete and appropriate for three, but that same child will need different information at age eight or twelve or sixteen.

As she grows, a child also begins to experience and understand more of the ways that the loss of the important person has and will continue to affect her life. While a four year-old misses Mommy, as she reaches different milestones in her life and development, she will re-experience what it means to miss her mother.

Some of the times/events that trigger re-grieving in children are:

- Reaching new stages in cognitive (intellectual) development.

- Experiencing stress or another loss.

- Significant events – graduations, Confirmation or Bar or Bat Mitzvah, concerts, recitals, big games, birthdays, weddings, etc.

- Seeing other children (friends or family) with their loved ones at significant events or even in everyday situations.

When children are revisiting and re-grieving their loss, new or dormant feelings may emerge. The coping and support strategies suggested here will be helpful in responding to them. Active grieving comes and goes throughout a child's life and it helps us (and them) to recognize it when we see it. Talking, playing, weather, colors, opening the door to conversation, maintaining compassionate and clear expectations, recognizing the many faces of grief, and listening with our hearts – all the ways to help our kids manage the emotional experience of loss require patience and compassion. It isn't always easy: especially since (most of the time) we're also grieving our loss of someone who meant the world to us. But the work is well worth it in the long run, for both our kids and ourselves.

Children who can talk about their feelings, accept them, and manage them are happier and better able to adjust and cope with difficult situations. They're resilient, and that is what we hope for our kids – that they come through the experience of life-changing loss, becoming exactly who they are meant to be, comfortable and confident in their own strength and heart.

As we close, don't forget this important recipe:

THE INGREDIENTS FOR A RAINBOW ARE SUNSHINE — AND RAIN.

Our lives, and the weather, are funny that way.

CHAPTER 7

I GOT PLENTY OF CHANGE *(EVEN THOUGH I DIDN'T VOTE FOR IT)*

Lately, it seems that we're "voting for change" every election year.

When you're a person who's experienced life-changing loss, you may feel that you've actually had ENOUGH change to last you another four (and then some) years. Politicians seem to suggest that change is good. But sometimes the reality is that change is difficult and unwelcome – in other words, sometimes not so good. Ironically (and no matter how we feel about it), change is the constant in our lives, the one thing we can count on.

At times in our lives we initiate and welcome change, reaching for a new goal or "making a change for the better." At other times, we are very effective at adjusting and adapting ourselves as circumstances shift around us. Sometimes, however, we'd rather crawl under a rock than deal with the possibility that we're going to have to accommodate change yet again. As we watch our kids grieving and growing, we can't avoid or deny change. For children, change is an inherent part of their growth and development.

How children react and respond to change can be complicated. Most kids embrace and celebrate the changes that are happening to them. They like being bigger, stronger, smarter, and more independent. They don't necessarily like having more responsibilities or more homework.

Most children are invested in certain people and things staying exactly the same: they prefer that their parents not be different, that the relationships they really count on continue to support and sustain them, that holidays and traditions remain comfortingly familiar (and almost identical every year), and that their environment (home, school, extracurriculars, communities of worship, neighborhood, etc.) and routines are stable and manageable.

Kids like being "Masters of (their own) Universe." Even when they're balking at bedtime, complaining about Thursday being broccoli night, or whining that they're the only ones whose parent won't let them go to a PG-13 movie, most kids (even bigger ones) actually need – and want – structure and consistency in their lives. It helps them to feel secure and confident.

Nothing goes off like an atomic bomb of change, however, like the experience of life-changing loss in your immediate family. Instead of thinking about what's different when someone we share our lives with dies, it might be quicker to take note of what, if anything, is the same. Every grieving family experiences its own kind and degree of upheaval, but the changes for most grieving families are substantial and difficult. Look over the following "laundry list" of change and see how many apply to you and your kids.

Are there changes in your home?
- Changes in where you live
- Changes in who lives with you or who you live with
- Changes in your environment (re-decorating, getting rid of belongings or furniture, reassigning rooms, etc.)

Are there changes in your family's financial situation?
- Who works and is financially responsible for the family
- Issues about how money is spent
- Concerns about private school tuition or college
- Changes in vacation plans, holidays, birthdays

Have you and your children experienced significant changes in your relationships with others?
- People with whom you have become closer
- People with whom you have become more distant
- People who you now see more often than you did
- People you see much less or not at all
- New people in your life (a nanny, a parent's new friend, a counselor)

Have the kids experienced changes at school or in the educational plans you or they have?
- How they're focused (or not), learning (or not)
- Who helps with homework
- Who keeps in touch with school and/or attends the PTO or parent-teacher conferences
- Educational/career plans or goals that have changed

Are there changes that any of you have experienced in your health and emotional well-being?

- How often you get sick
- How tired you are
- How emotional, sad, angry, or frustrated you feel
- How relieved or peaceful you feel

Are there changes in any of the systems and supports that you and the kids count on?

- Your own or someone else's faith or spiritual beliefs have changed and/ or are different from the rest of the family
- New interests OR you have given up something that was once important to you
- A change in what you believe is most important
- Something new about yourself, your family, or life in general that you believe (or something you don't believe anymore)

This laundry list isn't comprehensive. It doesn't reflect all the everyday changes in responsibilities, meal planning and preparation, housework, laundry, chauffeuring, or managing social obligations and schedules. It doesn't begin to capture how fundamentally different we all are as grievers — all the many substantial changes in our emotions, responses, reactions, and relationships.

The most important thing to recognize is that, more often than not, you and the kids are navigating your ocean of change pretty well. Mostly you're all in clean (enough) clothes, relatively well-fed, sort-of rested, showing up for work and school, and have not yet been featured on Hoarders: Buried Alive. You deserve a lot of credit for how well you're managing, although your heroic efforts may go unrecognized by those who haven't walked a mile in your grief shoes.

The message about change is not that it's so overwhelming that you're bound to be overwhelmed. The fact is that you're doing a good job and should recognize and appreciate your resilience and flexibility, individually and as a family.

Figuring out how to handle difficult change can be — well, difficult. Chances are that every single person in your family has come up against some kind of change that's been frustrating or painful for him or her. So, even if you're managing change well, what do you do when you hit a "land mine of change?"

First, you and your child need to identify the particular issue that's creating the anger, frustration, or discomfort. You have to ask, because your assumption about what's difficult for your kid may be way off base. The next step is figuring out if what changed actually had to change.

Some things that change unintentionally can be "changed back" without too much uproar.

For example, if the bedtime ritual changed at the time of your important person's death, it might be fairly easy to get back to what's familiar by planning and making some extra time for tucking in. If the important person was part of the ritual, however, it could mean creating something new and then repeating it often enough that it becomes the "new normal." That's the third step in dealing with change: creating something new to count on.

Step four is acknowledging that some issues won't have an easy or immediate solution. "Making it better" involves talking, grieving what you miss that's no longer possible, and patience with each other and the situation. Some things just take time to get used to.

It's good to recognize the stresses and strains of change. Coping with change, and helping our kids manage change, requires understanding, tolerance, and patience. Keep in mind that change happens to all families, not just your grieving family. Change continues throughout our lives and getting good at navigating change is a valuable and necessary life skill. Finally, it's true that change can inspire us to grow and become more than we've been before.

But don't change too much. We like you just the way you are!

CHAPTER 8

SAFETY, SECURITY, SUPPORT

When we design creative arts projects for working with grieving children, we're always looking for good metaphors, for things that are representative symbols that kids can understand.

Several times we have used construction and things that are constructed – houses, bridges, towers – as symbols for support systems. A support system is all the people, activities, beliefs, organizations, and communities that help us feel connected and safe.

On a few occasions, we have used fences as a symbol of support. Fences have gotten a bad rap through the years. In his poem *Mending Wall*, Robert Frost disagrees heartily with the neighbor who insists that, "Good fences make good neighbors." For Frost, fences represent separation, alienation, and distrust. But there's another way to think about a fence: it can keep the good stuff safe inside and the bad stuff out.

Through the years, there have even been songs written about a house with a little white picket fence — "This is home. This belongs to me and this is where I belong." Every fence itself depends on a supportive structure: without one, a fence doesn't stay upright very long. So we're inviting you to think about a fence of your (and your kids') very own, using the supportive family, friends, activities, and systems (like school, police, fire or medical) of your life as the building materials.

After the death of someone who is central to our lives, it may be hard to feel safe, secure, or supported. Life itself seems chaotic – in the case of any death and even more if the loss was unexpected, complicated, or traumatic. Your surviving children are looking to you to restore their sense of security. Perhaps you've seen the famous PEANUTS™ cartoon in which Charlie Brown, after giving Snoopy a reassuring hug, returns to his bed in the dark and asks, "Who reassures the reassurer?"

And it's a good question. If you're the parent, it's probably going to be you. While you may be your child(ren)'s primary support, the good news is that you're not alone (even if you're feeling that way). It might be a good time to count up your assets, in terms of support, and help your kids to do the same.

We're not suggesting that we rush past or deny the devastating sadness and loneliness that accompanies the loss of our partner, our child(ren)'s parent, or our own child. This kind of loss changes our lives forever. But it's possible, and absolutely necessary, to create opportunities to recognize who and what is "in our corner," to explore new relationships and possibilities, and to build a new support structure under and around ourselves and our kids. So grab a board and start construction!

Almost all of us have relationships with friends and family. We may have hoped that folks would move in closer to us after our loss and been disappointed because that didn't actually happen. Sometimes family and friends seem to hang back, becoming more distant. Sometimes when people move in closer, it feels like they're trying to take over, as though they don't trust us to know what we need or what we need to do. Both situations are frustrating.

We suggest taking some time to think about what the folks around you are good at and then playing to their strengths. Most people are more willing to do the things they feel competent at doing. If your sister is a great cook, ask for meals. If your best friend (or someone at church or the PTO you may not know very well) is a great listener, bend her ear (but remember to give her a break and try to spread the venting around a bit). Ask the neighbor with the great lawn who offered, "Just let me know what I can do" to treat the lawn for weeds. Find another single parent you like and trust to trade off baby-sitting so both of you can get a break once in a while.

Avoid asking people to do things they don't like to do or aren't very good at. It's less frustrating for everyone. Asking for specific kinds of assistance may also keep some folks from getting too intrusive or bossy – and they may actually be helpful!

There are activities and organizations that can provide support for your grieving family. Many hospices offer grief support programs for children and families like yours. If you belong to a faith community, your place of worship may offer activities for both you and your kids that are fun or educational, affirming, and relatively inexpensive.

If your children are young, your family is probably part of a school community, and schools can offer support, as well as referrals to community resources for assistance – from counseling to child care to debt management. Your physician can be a valuable partner during this trying time, particularly if you're comfortable sharing the truth about how you're doing, physically and emotionally.

Community medical agencies, like hospitals, provide health and wellness days and educational events for adults and kids. Most police and fire departments have annual open houses and, along with being fun, visiting the people who take care of our community and keep us safe can feel very reassuring for grown-ups and kids alike.

Don't underestimate the value of belonging and common interests for children. It can be very affirming for kids to belong to a team, a dance group, a choir, or the Scouts. Being part of a group that revolves around a common activity reinforces us in many ways: we develop our abilities and competence; we learn to cooperate with and rely on others; we experience that others count on us as well.

We and our children can benefit from the security that a sensible degree of structure creates in our lives. Certainly the loss of someone who is central to our lives can make things topsy-turvy. Clean clothes, healthy meals, reasonable bedtimes, and keeping the health department away may feel overwhelming. It's OK to let things slip a bit, lowering our sometimes-unrealistic standards.

After a few weeks, however, chaos and disorganization can begin to add to a feeling of insecurity. We can help our kids, and ourselves, by providing structure, not imposing it. They may need smaller meals more often, extra cuddling, our patience as they struggle with focus and follow-through, and some lenience and understanding if grades take a temporary dip. Our kids, however, actually feel better, and safer, when they understand the expectations we have for them and when we help them maintain meaningful schedules and routines.

Generally, we're not promoters of simply "looking on the bright side." It's fine if you can pull it off, but the loss of someone so important to you and your children deserves to be acknowledged as the life-changing event that it is. Your sorrow deserves respect and recognition. Grief is not the enemy: it contains the seeds of its own healing and it has value in our human experience. And although all that is sacred and true, it doesn't hurt to take a moment each day, with our kids, to notice something positive. We don't need to, and shouldn't, be fake or distracting. When we're sad, we have a right to our sadness.

Even in our dark days, however, most of us have something we can acknowledge as hopeful or helpful. Perhaps someone was kind to us or complimentary, tonight's vegetable selection was carrots instead of cauliflower, or the last casserole that the neighbor brought over wasn't tuna. Maybe washing the underwear with a red shirt is more funny than catastrophic. Today might be a good day to remember to hug each other good night – and decide to make it a new family tradition every night.

We all create our sense of security and support every day – one brick, board, or rock at a time. It's one step today and another tomorrow. We can focus on what to do today to make our children's lives, and our own, warmer, safer, calmer, and more secure. Find others to help. Remember to look for something good in this, and every other, day. No matter what we don't have right now, we still have each other.

CHAPTER 9

MEMORIES — *THAT KEEP GOING, AND GOING, AND GOING...*

It's interesting that something that happened in the past, which is unalterable, can seem to shift and change with time.

We expect that different people will remember the same incident differently. Some of our most hilarious (or troublesome) family stories are funny (or troublesome) for just that reason. We understand that our own personal point of view affects how we remember an event. What's somewhat harder to figure out is how and why our own memories change: even precious memories we cherish can become somewhat faded, foggier, or turned around as time goes by.

Here are some interesting memory facts:

- Research shows that the more strongly we feel about a person or event, negatively or positively, the more likely we are to form a memory. An event that invokes extreme feelings of panic or fear, however, may be wiped out of our consciousness entirely.

- The most active time to form memories over the course of a lifetime is during the adolescent and young adult years (which explains why so many of us can't stop talking about high school or college – and also why those are our best stories).

- Sense memories – like the sound of a person's voice or their face – are the hardest to retain. When a scent triggers a memory through our sense of smell, however, that memory will probably be vivid and lasting.

- The more we make a memory into a story and the more words we attach to it, the more likely we are to remember it.

Despite all that we have learned about memory, what and why we remember is a great mystery.

One of the ironies about memory is that we tend to remember unusual events more easily and have a harder time remembering specifics of things that were "everyday." It's the simple, quiet memories of days spent in our normal routines — the things we did the most often — that can slip away almost unnoticed.

We're more likely to have a memory of a once-in-a-lifetime trip to Disney World than being able to recall the richness of the simple experiences we shared over and over again with someone important, the details of an "ordinary" day we spent with him or her. When someone important in our life dies, that can be a sad and painful reality.

Kids tell us that they worry when they can't "hear" the person's voice anymore or remember what they talked with him/her about on the drive to school or volleyball practice. Scrapbooks, photo albums, and videos can spark and enliven our memories, but we tend to confine our use of media to the big events. Do any of us have video of a Tuesday morning breakfast or a Saturday afternoon at the mall? We probably have more now, thanks to cellphones, but those need to be conscientiously backed-up or they may irrevocably disappear.

Memories are like muscles; we have to "use 'em or lose 'em." It takes a conscious effort to hold onto memories, especially for our children. For people of any age, the way to retain a memory is to first think about the memory as a story of a specific event. We can't remember every Friday "pizza and movie night" so we have to reconstruct a particular or particular few Friday night "pizza and movie" memory(ies).

The next step is putting words to the "memory story" – describing the event in the same sequence, using the same words, almost like a script or the words of a favorite book. (Who doesn't remember the first few lines of *The Cat in the Hat, Where the Wild Things Are,* or *Goodnight, Moon*?) To hold onto the memory, we, and our kids, need to hear and tell those important memories the same way, time after time.

Over time, hearing the memory creates specific pictures in our minds and "seeing" those pictures played repeatedly gives them life, vividness, and detail. The familiar story also inspires feelings in our hearts and the feelings become attached to the memory. **The more words, images, and feelings we connect to the memory, the more staying power the memory has.**

If we want to remember what it felt like to be with someone we've loved, especially when we can't be with them anymore, it takes intention and effort to create the kind of memories that we can hang our hearts on. For our kids, memories are too important to be left entirely to chance.

Some kids were too young (or weren't even around) to have any personal memories of the important person who died. Sharing stories helps them to develop a sense of connection, understanding better whose child (or brother, sister, granddaughter, or nephew) they are. Littler kids often "insert" themselves in the story, taking on a role that may be mostly imaginary, and that's just fine. It's easier to hold on to something when you see and feel yourself as part of it.

Especially precious for our children are their special memories of "you and me" – those memories that strongly evoke a sense of togetherness and connection with the important person who died. Since it's really in the everyday conversation and routine where we can "find" the person we've lost and our relationship with him or her, it's important to foster specific memories of being together. Memories of activities they shared, times of day when they felt especially connected, cuddling, wrestling, helping with homework, learning to ride a bike — things that were just between the two of them are very important. Helping kids to retain "you and me" memories strengthens their sense of that unique relationship.

Some of us have concerns about difficult memories that our kids are carrying around. There may have been times when their important person was difficult, impatient, or angry due to physical or mental illness. A long dying process can have many powerful and frightening passages. Sudden death can be traumatic, associated with troubling images and sounds. The darker side of memory can make our children anxious and us anxious for them.

We can't erase difficult memories for our children or for ourselves. It's much more useful to help our kids understand their difficult memories and balance them. Knowing what was happening at a frightening time often takes some of the "scary" out of the event.

For very little ones, a resuscitation attempt could look like somebody was beating their important person. Explaining that "the man that pounded on Daddy's chest when he was lying on the floor was trying to help make Daddy's heart beat again," even though it didn't work, can take some misunderstanding and fear out of the memory.

Being told that "Grandma was cranky because she was uncomfortable and couldn't sleep, but, even when she was angry, she still loved you," can help a child who might feel that he had done something wrong to provoke the anger. It's also important for kids to understand that "we all (even grown-ups) cry when we're sad, but we won't always be this sad – and, no matter what, we can still take care of you."

To balance difficult memories we first help our kids to acknowledge, express, and understand the hard (or bad) memories. Our children also need to be told that their responses to a difficult situation or memory of it are understood and accepted. Children need to understand that it's okay to feel angry at (or disappointed with or tired of) someone you love – that happens to everyone sometimes. Little guys also need to be told that being mad or thinking bad thoughts about someone cannot and did not hurt the person or make something bad happen to him/her.

The next step is to revisit and share more positive memories and stories to create a balanced picture of our important person who died and our child's relationship with him/her – "Sometimes Daddy was mad and loud when he felt bad, but I remember when he took you to ballet class and told you how beautiful you were when you danced. Do you remember that?"

Memories are sometimes difficult, sometimes warm and fuzzy, sometimes dramatic and often elusive – but they are the stuff that a sense of belonging, an understanding of yourself, and never-ending love are made of. Our children's hearts and lives are richer when they can recall the journey, "remembering when you walked with me — and knowing that you always will."

CHAPTER 10

"WINNING" THE COMMUNICATION GAME

Communicating with our kids isn't actually a game, but when communication works well, everybody wins.

When it's not going so well, it seems like everybody loses. Navigating both our children's grief experience and our own, finding common ground, compromising, adjusting, and establishing new rules for our new and different family are complicated issues. This requires more advanced communication skills than we, and our children, have developed to this point.

Although we may not understand the rules about communicating at "the top of our game," it's often pretty clear when an unspoken rule gets broken — and someone winds up fouled out or in the penalty box!

So, are there rules for good communication around tough issues? We'd actually prefer to think in terms of **guidelines and ideas about how to manage and improve communication** in our families.

Our first suggestion is a very old one: unless what your child is doing could involve serious bodily harm, **take 5 seconds and a deep breath before yelling**. It's amazing how much more logical and controlled you can sound in five short seconds. We're modeling better communication for our kids when we're responding to what's going on instead of simply (and loudly) reacting.

Have you ever noticed how noise escalates? Parties and restaurants provide powerful examples of how people get louder and louder in a noisy environment. At some point, when assaulted by loud noise, most of us become overwhelmed and tune out. We don't want to inadvertently train our kids to ignore requests or directions given in a conversational tone and then to react only to our angry, agitated, and loud voice. Our homes are a lot more peaceful if there's less yelling and then, if we choose to raise our volume *occasionally*, we are more likely to get someone's attention.

Speaking of habits (or ingrained behaviors), chances are good that our kids have developed some that can drive us to distraction. Before throwing in the towel or making even more (and louder) unanswered demands, have we tried to **"catch him (or her) being good?"** Incentives to get things accomplished and praise when that happens can turn the whole "push-pull" process around for a kid. This second guideline is actually based on an old axiom from our great- grandmothers: "You catch more flies with honey than vinegar." More positive words and positive experiences mean more good communication — and kids who are more willing to talk and cooperate with us.

A third guideline for communication is to model respect. Our kids should respect us. Clearly, most kids will cross the line on occasion (and some have developed some pretty snotty habits). It's tempting to pull out the "I'll tell you why — because I'm your parent" card or to "show them their place." We are bigger (most of us), stronger, and in charge. Here's something else your mother was right about: **don't stoop to someone's (current) level of behavior**.

Continuing to respond as though you are worthy of respect and expressing disappointment that your child would choose to do less has much more impact than a shouting match. Sometimes a kid is being a brat, but it's best to keep it to ourselves and avoid name-calling or anything that defines and identifies the child by his or her undesirable behavior.

A fourth guideline is that we can affirm feelings, without affirming unacceptable behavior. If your grieving child is acting up, it may be an expression of his or her grief. Bereaved kids are often something besides sad: their grief may get expressed as anger, frustration, inattention, recklessness, irritability, or despair.

If your child is acting out, it can help to name the feeling and affirm it, before addressing the behavior that has to stop.

> *"It seems like you're angry, very angry. I know that you're disappointed that we're not going to do what you'd like to do right now. But you seem angrier than that. Sometimes, since Dad died, I feel very angry too and I try not to take that out on you and other people I love. Angry is OK, but _____ (yelling, using bad words, hitting, demanding your own way, calling names) is not OK. There are things to do about feeling angry. Can you think of some?"*

End the conversation with a review of what we are not going to do and what is OK to do.

The reverse of this situation is when your kid is playing the "grief card." He or she has been reprimanded and then starts "whiny-crying," saying, "I miss

Mommy." Certainly, a child can be missing Mommy and feeling quite badly. But chances are we've also seen a kid looking for an acceptable reason for an unacceptable behavior or reaction. It's OK to let them know that we all miss Mommy sometimes, but right now it seems like he or she is unhappy about _____ and we need to talk about that. End the conversation by reassuring your child that you will always be ready to talk with him or her about Mommy or hard feelings.

These strategies may sound pretty basic — and they are. But the guidelines aren't just for little kids. They go for our big kids as well. A very wise mother of a *Good Mourning* teen once said to her parent group, "I don't always know if the mouthiness, eye-rolling, and laziness is grief or being 15, but some things just have to stop." And she was right.

On the positive side is more positive communication — the things that encourage our kids to see us as the person they can go to, someone who is squarely and reliably in their corner. A lot of positive communication with our children begins with less talking on our part and more really listening to them.

Resist the urge to jump into the conversation or interrupt. Sometimes we get ahead of our kids, seeing the trouble in the troubling story before they get to the end.

Reflect back to them what you heard, letting them know that you understand what the problem was for them in the situation.

Ask if they have any ideas on how you could help and then do as they ask or re-frame how you could be of assistance, if their solution is not an acceptable or effective one.

Affirm how your child feels before you point out how her words and actions may have affected others or been received by them.

Trust that your child's intentions are good, but if you really see a problem, ask how he might have responded if he were the other person or people involved.

Sometimes, it's helpful to let your child tell you what's happening and then tell her that you will think about what was shared and get back to her in a little while. It helps you to have some time to **be thoughtful in your response**. It also helps your child to know that you're taking his issues very seriously. One note — the younger your child, the less she can tolerate not getting an immediate response, so this is mostly for bigger kids with bigger kid issues.

Sharing, active listening, defining challenges and problems, and reasoning together to get to a workable solution in which everyone is a stakeholder — is respectful and effective communication at its best. Like with everything else, we and our kids will sometimes rise to the occasion and sometimes miss the mark entirely. Great parenting is about intention, thoughtfulness, and being a good example — not about demanding perfection from our kids or ourselves.

By the way, a little "volume" now and then never hurt anybody. Italian families like mine have known this for years!

CHAPTER 11

LIFE GOES ON...

Since the death of someone important to you and your children, you may have heard that phrase more than you can stand.

It's so obvious — yes, everything goes on, rushing past. And what is so magical about time going on when it feels like we're leaving someone we've loved very much, someone who has been important in our life — behind?

The other side of the passage of time is that we see our kids continually grieving and growing. We worry when they struggle and we enjoy and take pride in their learning and their accomplishments. As we move farther down the road in own our grief journey, we may notice that we're getting a little stronger, a little more organized, a little better able to catch a glimpse of our vision and hopes for our family's future. As it always has been, life going on is a mixed bag. We're always having to say goodbye to something familiar to move onto welcoming something new.

Our children may be powerful reminders of what was good (or not so good) about the people we've lost — and about ourselves too. Kids who've experienced the death of a sibling can remind of us of the child who's died and of what our family used to be. Whether it's the loss of a parent, a grandparent, a sibling, or another significant person, we can be sure that the person who died left their mark on our children.

A kid's curly hair, blue eyes, incredibly skinny ankles, or dimple can bring our loved one to mind. Sometimes the resemblance takes us by surprise — when we see the child out of the corner of our eye or come upon an old picture of our loved one that looks like our child does today. It may be a mannerism, an inflection, an expression, or the sound of our teen's (changing) voice that reminds us.

A quick temper, a love of animals, an outrageous sense of humor, an amazing singing voice all illustrate, time and again, that life does in fact, go on. And, in us, so do the folks we've loved and lost.

Genetics isn't the only way our children are connected to the important people in their lives who've died. Adopted kids or kids in blended families have powerful attachments and connections to the people who have loved and cared for them. What our kids turn out to be is partly "nature," but it's "nurture" as well: whoever lives with children every day, raises them, and teaches them leaves an imprint on them and lives on in them too.

When we consider our children and their place on our family tree, we recognize all the complex connections that define belonging to a family. Inherited traits and how we're biologically related is only part of our tree, and perhaps not the most important part. It's important to help our kids recognize all kinds of connections to others, including talents, interests, and lessons they've learned from the important people in their lives.

Make some time to talk with your kids about who they're connected to, who they're like, who they've learned from, and who loved them — and loves them still. Make note of similarities to the important people that you've loved and share those with them. Speak truthfully and compassionately about character strengths and flaws, both those of the important person who died and their own as well. Share precious stories.

Although we often concentrate on the *things* that people leave behind after their death, the most powerful legacy is found in the hearts and minds of those of us who live on – and, in us and through us, their legacy lives on as well.

In the book *Dandelion Wine* by Ray Bradbury, an elderly character facing her death says: "I'm not really dying today. No one ever died who had a family." It's good to know that life goes on and with it connection, caring, love — and sometimes dimples.

"WHOMEVER YOU'VE BEEN THINKING ABOUT, WHETHER THEY'RE HERE OR FAR AWAY OR EVEN IN HEAVEN, IMAGINE HOW PLEASED THEY'D BE TO KNOW YOU RECOGNIZE WHAT A DIFFERENCE THEY'VE MADE IN YOUR BECOMING."

– Mr. Fred Rogers

CHAPTER 12

SOMETIMES IT ISN'T THE EARTHQUAKE, IT'S THE AFTERSHOCKS

When we experience life-changing loss, we may approach the experience with certain expectations — particularly if it's our first encounter with deep grief.

Most of us expect that somehow we'll get better. We know that it will take time and that the road won't be an easy one. Most of us believe, however, that the road leads upward and that once recovery and adjustment begins, it will continue.

When we take the long view, it's probably true that the passage of time and the work we do to achieve our "new normal" will come together to move us forward. When we're in deep and early grief, however, we can be surprised at how bumpy and up-and-down the road actually is. For our kids, the initial impact of the loss of their important person takes a great toll, but the unanticipated changes they have to deal with as time goes on often cause new sadness and disappointment.

Within a very few weeks or months after a death occurs — particularly the loss of a spouse/parent — we, as adults, begin to understand that many things in our lives may have to change. Routines are different and finances may be different. Perhaps relocating is necessary.

Along with the impact of the loss in very concrete ways, we are thinking about how the absence of our important person will affect our hopes and dreams for the future, our own and our children's. We understand that our partner won't be there for confirmations, graduations, choosing a college, the walk down the aisle.

Those realities, however, tend to occur to children as time goes on and they experience these as unwelcome surprises, new losses, and more disappointment. Many grieving children have expressed that the latest manifestation of the loss came as a nasty shock to them, just when they were starting to feel hopeful again. Sometimes, it isn't the earthquake...

Since hoping and wishing are often associated with Santa Claus, tooth fairies, and birthday candles, we might lose sight of how important they are in our children's lives. Just as learning is a critical part of children's development, so is the act of hoping and wishing. For children, hopes and wishes provide a focus for being and becoming. Even fantastic and unrealistic visions that seem unlikely or implausible have a purpose, fueling a child's sense of great possibility.

It's important for children to be hopeful. Hopefulness is an attitude of expectation and possibility. Hope allows us to believe that what we want can be achieved and that things will turn out positively. Children need hope to make positive steps into their own futures. So how do we help our kids to hold onto hope? How can we help them develop a positive vision of their tomorrows? How do we help them tolerate the after-shocks of grief and become resilient?

For most children, and perhaps even more so for bereaved children, reality will close in (or has closed in) soon enough. Bereaved children often feel more vulnerable than children who have not had to face the reality of life-changing loss. Bereaved children have experienced great disappointment. They have seen that very bad things can happen to very good people, in direct opposition to what they may have been taught about the rewards of doing good.

In the face of this reality, hopes and wishes can seem tenuous at best. It is often adolescents who are most likely to consider hopes and wishes childish and irrelevant. Ironically, they are the ones for whom investing in tomorrow is most critical, as they stand on the threshold of making very important decisions that will shape their futures.

Hopes and wishes are not exclusively the business of kids, however. Even we grown-ups carry cherished hopes — for ourselves certainly, and often even more for our children. When a family confronts life-changing loss, hope can feel like a stretch for everybody. As parents, our job is to help our kids reach for hope, to face their own futures with a sense of possibility. That's a big job, but we can start by taking some very small steps.

First, acknowledge that you're all sad and that it's tough to be hopeful. Then begin to talk about a time in the future, when things, and all of you, will be better. Simple statements like, "I know we won't always be this sad" or "No matter what, I'll always take care of you" can go a long way in easing stress for kids and helping them feel more secure and certain that they'll be all right. Please understand that your expressions of hope — even if you're operating in the "fake it 'til you make it" mode — are very reassuring for your kids.

Second, it's important to help our children develop a realistic sense about their lives. While everything may not be good all the time, it isn't all bad either. It's helpful to recognize and take note of the good things — a great dinner, a better grade, help from friends, kindness from people around us, security where we find it, something that we're good at or that we enjoy.

Catch your kids being good and point it out to them. Be appreciative of their successes, even the little ones. We know that negativity can be self-perpetuating, an attitude that affects not only our expectations, but also our perception of events (the "glass half empty" mind-set). Practicing positivity and hopefulness has a similarly powerful, and opposite, effect.

Finally, help your kids focus on something that they can look forward to and then make sure it happens. Disney World is something to look forward to, but so is a great day at the zoo, and the zoo might be much more possible now. The most important thing is not how spectacular the plan, but rather that it's achievable. Children need to see that there are things they can count on, so we should avoid over-promising and under-delivering whenever possible. Our reliability restores their confidence that they can wish and hope and anticipate good things and those things will happen.

It's important to expect and understand that our kids will experience new consequences of their loss over time: they may never have seen a particular disappointment (no Mom at Confirmation, picking out a college without Dad, going off to high school as an "only" without the older brother or sister) or set-back coming, even though we did. This is normal, something that is bound to happen at times. Understanding and anticipating that this will happen can make it less overwhelming to us. When we're not feeling blind-sided, we have more confidence in our children's ability to get through the difficult passage and in our ability to support them as they do.

Hope for our children is not just a matter of good or bad luck; it's not something that children develop only when everything goes well. When difficult things occur, like life-changing loss, their hope doesn't have to desert them. Hope is not about what happens or doesn't happen; it's about our confidence in our own ability to handle difficulties and persevere until a time when things take a turn for the better. It's about understanding and believing that our lives and we ourselves are full of potential.

A few lines from the movie *The Best Exotic Marigold Hotel* provide us with a significant (and very condensed) lesson about the nature of hope:

IN INDIA, WE HAVE A SAYING, "EVERYTHING WILL BE ALL RIGHT IN THE END." SO IF IT IS NOT ALL RIGHT, IT IS NOT YET THE END.

CHAPTER 13

HO, HO, OH NO:
SURVIVING THE HOLIDAYS

From the end of October when they're dressing up as super heroes, princesses, and goblins until they fall asleep in front of the TV at 11:45 on December 31st, our kids (especially the littler ones) are enthusiastically in the holiday mode.

While their joyful anticipation can be quite inspiring, it may present a real challenge as well.

Finding our way through the holidays after the experience of life-changing loss can feel like navigating a rough, windswept journey at sea — setting our sails in one direction and then having to realign them, wondering if we're sailing in the right direction at all, tiring of the storms and waves, and hoping for rest and that we get safely to shore. We want to get to the end of the holiday season with a minimum of chaos and disappointment. Our children want everything to be the way it used to be and they can be very anxious or sad when things are different.

The newly bereaved among us are looking for answers, for ideas, for direction, for peace. For those of us who have already been through a holiday season without our loved one, things may seem a little more familiar. We have found our way once — or more times than that — and we're learning what works (and doesn't) for ourselves and our children. Perhaps we even find ourselves joining our kids in renewed and child-like hope.

Wherever you find yourself this year, we're wishing you a blessed holiday season. Chances are good, however, that it will require some forethought and planning to put the "Thanks" in your Thanksgiving, the "Happy" in your Hanukkah, and the "Merry" in your Christmas. We recommend taking some time to talk with your kids, negotiating a little (or a lot), planning, and flexibility: it's as important as cookie-baking, gift wrapping, and light-stringing for getting through to New Year's Day with the most peace and least panic.

The first item on the holiday agenda is **permission** — permission to miss what used to be, permission to change things that need to be different, permission to change things back at a later date, and permission to adapt and change your plans when necessary.

The second item is **anticipating what is different** without the important person who died, in both the practical and profound sense. Who covers the things he or she used to do to get ready for the holidays, or do we let some of that go this year? Making a list and deciding together, as a family, what is really important, what can wait for another year, and what really doesn't matter all that much can bring clarity to the process of getting ready.

You may arrive at a much clearer sense of what is important to each member of the family and be surprised at all the busy work that you can avoid. Even when all the tasks are accounted for (and some eliminated), there remains the absence of your very important person that hangs over the holidays, bringing us to third item on our agenda.

The third item is finding a way to **memorialize** and include your loved one in your traditions and celebrations. Ritual helps to bring a sense of remembrance and peace out of our pain. There are many home-grown rituals that can be helpful — hanging the loved one's stocking and filling it with notes or donations to charity, setting his place at the table, a special ornament, or anything else that your family traditionally associates with him.

A word about visits to the cemetery at this time of year: visiting the cemetery can be an important way to remember or include your loved one and it may be essential for your family, but don't take everybody out to the cemetery on Christmas Eve, Christmas Day, the afternoon of the 1st Night, or any other time **just because you feel it's expected**. While healing and helpful for some, for others a visit to the cemetery is very draining and would be best done a few days before or after the actual holiday. People, especially our children, have a right to unadulterated happiness in the moments they can experience it.

All the usual rules apply during the holidays. Kids do best with a **sensible schedule** (item four on the holiday agenda), good diet, downtime, and playtime. The holidays have a way of testing and stretching our best intentions to maintain routine and practical schedules: after all, the holidays are, by definition, days that aren't like every other day.

This is where item five on the agenda — **flexibility and patience** — comes into play. Not all our plans, no matter how well-considered, will become reality. People, big and little, can get tired, sad, overwhelmed, over-sugared, and "bah-humbugged." Sometimes there is nothing like a good cry, a big hug, an early bedtime, or some peace and quiet. If you miss something this year, there's always next year!

The same things that your family is learning to do to manage the demands of every ordinary day will help with the holidays. Communication is key, acknowledging the changes in your family is essential, making time to remember feeds the soul, and patience conquers all. A great big dose of "able to laugh at ourselves" helps as well. Here's to you and your kids — to every day that you've survived, every accomplishment, every act of strength and compassion, every time you chose hope in the face of despair. And here's to perseverance!

NOTES

ABOUT THE AUTHOR

Vicki Scalzitti is the Manager of Family and Community Education at Rainbow Hospice and Palliative Care. For more than 25 years, Vicki has been working to support grieving children and adults through their experiences of life-changing loss.

In addition to her work with the Good Mourning Program at Rainbow Hospice and Palliative Care, Vicki is an accredited crisis and trauma specialist, serving local area schools and organizations through Rainbow's *Grief in Schools* support program.

Vicki and her family suffered a personal loss in 1989 with the accidental drowning of her five-year-old son, Joey. Since that time, she has dedicated herself to building and creating resources for grieving families and sharing her experience in helping others cope with grief.

In addition to *The Road to Good Mourning*, Vicki is also the co-author of *10 Steps for Parenting Your Grieving Children* with Dr. Anne Hatcher Berenberg and Jack Cain. She is also a nationally recognized speaker on children's grief issues.